CHANGING YOUR LIFE FOR THE BETTER

BY. JERRELL A. GOODEN

Table of Contents

Prologue

1. What is Change- pg. 1

2. Having a Positive Mindset- pg. 7

3. Listening to Positive People- pg. 13

4. Learning what you purpose is- pg. 18

5. Never Limit Yourself- pg. 27

6. Having faith in God- pg. 34

7. Learning how to deal with change- pg. 39

8. Knowing when to change- pg. 48

9. Going after the life you want- pg. 55

10. Bettering yourself- pg. 63

11. Encouraging others in a positive way- pg. 72

12. Taking responsibility for your actions- pg. 77

13. Create a positive routine- pg. 81

14. Set realistic goals- pg. 87

15. Rid your life of negativity- pg. 94

16. Putting God first in anything you set your mind to- pg. 101

17. Leaving the past where it is- pg. 109

18. Pay more attention to your life- pg. 118

19. Don't stress over what you can't control- pg. 122

20. Invest in yourself- pg. 131

21. Care less of what people may think of you- pg. 140

22. Final Thoughts on Everything- pg. 150

dedication

To all my siblings

I love every one of you all, and I really thank them for making me the man that I am today; God bless every one of you all. I couldn't ask for better siblings.

PROLOGUE

This book is going to be about how and when it is necessary to start making changes to your life for the better. Me as the author of this book will be talking about what change is and will also be describing the meaning of this term in my own words. Change can be good sometimes; however, it can also be a bad thing to experience if you're not ready for it when it comes.

In addition to what I am going to be talking about is having that positive mindset that things will work out in the long run. Change can be a hard and tough thing to go through, but I feel that it is important to learn how to evolve and change with the times for the better. We all will have to do it eventually because technology is getting more and more advanced and some of the old ways of doing things are going to be a thing of the past.

I will be talking about how to have the confidence as well as the faith that we must have to change your life in a positive way. It is a must to have the faith that things are going to work in your favor. Life has a lot of positive things to offer. It is up to us to either take advantage of it or let the things that can help make our lives better just go by. Life is about taking chances and risk because if you don't take risk, you will be stuck in the same cycle or rut for the rest of your life.

Another thing that we need to know in life before we start to make changes in it is our purpose. I will really be going to into depth about that topic because to make the positive move in your life, in my opinion it is a requirement to know what your purpose is. Your purpose can be anything from being a preacher or just a factory worker just to name a couple of things. I strongly believe that everyone has a destiny to fore fill in life. life is too short to be scared to take chances or make the necessary changes in your life for the better.

Among the other things that I will be talking about is trying to have that positive mindset in any and everything that you may attempt to accomplish in your lifetime. It is critical to make sure that you have that positive mindset. When have a positive mindset, you must surround yourself with positive people.

Changing your life for the better may sometimes affect the people around you in a negative way, but to keep your peace intact you must have that strong mindset that you will secede in anything that you are trying to accomplish in life. Some people may not like the person that you are becoming, but if you're not mistreating people in the process of this positive change in your life keep doing you until you accomplish your goal that you may want to achieve. Success does not come easy in life; it is just like that old saying to get something you never had you have to do something you have never done. Changing your life in a positive way can be one of the best things you could ever do. To conclude this introduction to this book I will also be talking about some of the challenges that you may have to face to make them certain changes and apply them to life situations. Some people don't like change however, it is a part of growing up and being an adult. Well, I hope whoever is reading this book will take some of the things that I am saying and apply them to their life. I am not an expert on these things, I am just going by my personal experiences that I have encountered in my life. I hope everyone that is reading this book will enjoy it.

CHAPTER

1

WHAT IS CHANGE

T he true meaning of the word change is defined as to make (someone or something) different; alter or modify. The second definition of the word change is to replace (something) with something else, especially something of the same kind that is newer or better; substitute one thing for (another). Now that I have defined the meaning of the word change, I am going to explain this in my own words. How I define the word change is to try to evolve and alternate and trying to better yourself in a positive way in life. Life can take you a lot of places rather in a positive or a negative way. I am not going to say that change isn't for everyone, however it can be a beneficial thing for you in the future.

I am going to use the word technology as an example. Technology has evolved over the years especially on how we communicate with one another. Also, technology can be misused in many ways, and it can create chaos and cause unnecessary grief to be added to our lives. Technology can also be an asset in our lives when it is used in the correct way. Times are changing. I feel that if we don't learn how to adapt or adjust to the things that are changing, we can get lost in the shuffle. If everything stayed the same all the time, it would be a tough and boring world that we would be living in. Sometimes we must make that necessary change to get to that next important level that is required in life.

My mother always told me that you can either change for the lifestyle that you may want, or you can stay in that same rut and be miserable. Some of the people that stay in the same rut and trying to be resistance to change be the main ones that be either complaining all the time or blaming others for their current situation that they may be in. I remember listening to Steve Harvey and he said some things that really hit home for me personally, the things that he said is that for us to be successful in life you will have to jump.

Steve Harvey didn't mean jump literally off a cliff; he was talking about metaphorically. The meaning that I interpret from his video was you can't stay in your comfort zone and expect a different thing to happen to you all the time. You are going to have some hardships and setbacks during your life journey especially going after the life you may want. It is ok to play it safe sometimes, however you may miss your blessing if you choose to give up on the positive lifestyle that you are going after. I had found myself playing it safe on many occasions. I am going to use getting my driver's license as one of my examples. I didn't get my driver's license until I was 28 years old, and I am not ashamed to admit it. People may laugh at me, but I don't care because they don't know the hard work that went into it especially when your mother doesn't have a car to practice in. One night after work I was talking to mom about it and she said, ***"don't be discourage do your best and let God do the rest."*** I had it in my mind that I was going to praise God rather I pass the driver's test or not.

I realized that for me to make this a reality I had to change my thinking and step out of my comfort zone by boldly asking my preacher could I practice in his car. I just got tired of feeling sorry for myself just for the fact that I didn't have my license, so I decided that one day I am going to change this feeling. I went to the armory and took the test and past it with an 81 percent. I was so excited that I ran around in the park like a little kid, and to be honest I was more excited that I finally got my license than me getting my first car. I thanked my preacher for sticking by me and everything. The moral of the story that I just told you all is don't be afraid to get out your comfort zone occasionally. Also, we need to learn that God is in control, and anything is possible through him.

CHAPTER

2

HAVING A POSITIVE MINDSET

Having that positive mindset when it comes to changing your life for the better is a very important asset to have about yourself. My mother always told me to have an open mind about things and people. As for me personally, I try not to judge people from what others either say about them or what they do. Rather you are rich or poor we are not any better than the next person.

God wants us to have that positive mindset when you are trying to make that big change in a positive way. It is important to put God first in all the things that we may do in life. like I said before God is in control of all things. I refuse to stress over things that I have no control over, however that is easier said than done especially when you're still young. I love God and a firm believer in what he can do for me as well as anyone else. God always says if you ask in his name you shall receive. God has helped me and my family in some tough situations throughout my life.

Another way to have that positive mindset when it comes to changing your life in a positive way is to keep your negative thoughts to a minimum. Sometimes, keeping them bad thoughts to a minimum can be a challenge. It can be something to struggle with daily, but as for me personally I try to keep a smile on my face every day because God wants us to be happy. When you start thinking bad thoughts about taking a certain risk that can benefit you, you can miss your blessing from God.

When I was young, I would think about bad thoughts all the time when it came to taking chances in life. When I got older, I would think things through before I take that chance because there are consequences in anything we do in life rather they're good or bad. Overthinking all the time can do something to you in a psychological way and I am not talking about in a positive way. I personally tend to overthink a lot myself. As we get older you are going to mature and sometimes have them negative thoughts in your mind. Stepping out of your comfort zone can be an overwhelming thing to do especially if it is for the first time in your life. I had to realize that it was something I had to do for me to get what I either needed or wanted in life. I honestly think that I get that overthinking trait from my late mother because she was careful on the things that she may say or do.

Practicing positive self-talk can be one of the starting points to use when you are trying to make them necessary changes in your life. Some people may find this weird, but I do talk to myself daily especially when I am at work. I mean you must keep yourself entertained in some way so to speak. We must have that self-talk occasionally; you also can't fear what people may think about you.

To practice good self-talk, you must first think about the things to be thankful for in life. Me in a personal level I am thankful that I have my freedom and God has given me another chance to get closer to him. Being thankful for the simple things in life is one of the key things to do when you are on your way to changing your life in a positive way.

You must be open to humor in relax when trying to do things that are positive. Laugh sometime, shoot the breeze, and enjoy life. Sometimes I could be at work doubting myself and all the sudden I just start smiling because of a good, funny, or positive memory comes to my mind.

I think when we laugh about certain things it can relieve some stress that we may be going through. Laughing is an important and fun thing to do when life gives you lemons so to speak. I have seen and met some of the most less fortunate people that are just as happy and in good spirits, and as far as some rich people, it's sometimes the exact opposite. You can have all the money in the world and not be happy. I much rather be poor, laughing, and happy than rich and miserable. I try my best every day to be happy and having that positive mindset is a crucial asset to have as far as making the positive changes in your life.

CHAPTER

3

LISTENING TO POSITIVE PEOPLE

When you are trying to make them certain changes to your life, must learn how to listen and be around positive people. I often think about all the elders that I have personally encountered over the years, some of them were a good influence in my life. You also have certain people in life that are negative and give off a bad vibe when you encounter them. The best thing to do when someone comes at you in a negative way is to shun them and tune them out. Some people that way may listen to may not have our best interest at heart, and I think that is why God has given us five senses.

When I was growing up, I did have some teachers and church members that were in my corner. The thing about me is that I don't mind anybody hurting my feelings when it comes to telling me the truth because that means that they care and have your best interest at heart. We must listen to positive people to make them positive changes in our life. My mom used to tell me stories about how she was around older people when she was growing up that were trying to tell her the right way to go in life. We all need help occasionally. As a child growing up, I was often afraid to ask others for help or advice. I was just a shy kid growing up trying to figure certain things out on my own. One of the elders that I went to church with just told me, when you need help don't be too proud to say anything. I had to learn that in the process of growing into an adult. Even with me being in my 30s I am still somewhat shy and afraid to ask for either advice on certain things of just need help doing something.

God put certain people in our lives for a reason. I think that the negative people are just a lesson that we will have to learn because God puts us to the test each day of our lives. Every day when we wake up in the morning our souls are at stake.

Don't let negative people try to influence you into doing something bad because they are miserable themselves. When you are around

negative people all the time, you pick up some of

their ways and bad habits. I recall when I graduated

college people were asking me why I am working

in a factory; I told them if only you knew my

circumstances you would understand.

Then I thought about the reply I just gave to

that person, and I thought I don't owe them

anything or any kind of explanation at all; I mean

we are all here trying to make a living and earn

money for ourselves and family. You also got

certain people with negative mindsets and try to

make fun of you and discourage you when you are

trying to do something positive with your life

because their lives are all messed up and

everything. Then you have them certain people that don't want to see you make it or fail at what you are trying to accomplish. I am trying each day to listen to the positive people that are trying to show me the right direction to go by doing the things that I need to do to become successful.

CHAPTER
4

LEARNING WHAT YOU PURPOSE IS

When we start to figure out what our purpose is in life, then you start to get a since of direction. Making positive changes in your life can be challenging at times, however the work that you may be putting in to making it happen will pay off if you stay persistent about what you want to do. It took me a while and I am still trying to find out what my purpose is in life. Do not get me wrong I do have certain goals that I want to achieve but finding direction can be a challenge sometimes.

I remember when I was in the fourth grade

and had college on my mind at that age and didn't even know what college was all about or anything. I said to myself that I am going to get into college one day; I didn't know how but I just had that ambition that I was going to go. College was a great experience for me at the time that I went. I've met all kinds of people rather they were good or bad, but I didn't just get an education out of it, I experienced a taste of what the world was going to be like in my future.

One of the tools that you can use to try to figure out what your purpose is in life would be to identify the things that you may care about. I also think that this is a good asset to have when you are on your way to making them positive changes to your life. I honestly think that God has blessed everyone to has a hidden talent that we may not know about. Sometimes the hobbies that we may do in our spare time can become a part of making a living for ourselves. It is kind of like a side hustle that you may do and before long you can start to love and get so good at it that it can become your permanent job.

When you are trying to find your purpose in life, never leave a stone unturned. When you find something that you may care about, you can use that as fuel to set the tone in trying to find out what's your purpose in life. You must have that certain starting point as far as creating a foundation for yourself.

Recognizing your strengths and talents can

also be another tool to use when moving in the right direction in life. No one is the best at everything. We all have our strengths and weaknesses. Some people may be great at things like sports, video games, or just inventing things, but the point that a am trying to make is God has different plans and ideas for us all. God knows what our strengths and talents are, it is up to us to find them and use them in a positive way. I have seen some people firsthand with all the talent in the world waste it because they are either afraid that they won't secede or make a huge mistake that may derail them from using that talent that they acquired over the years. It is just like that old saying goes, "a good mind is a terrible thing to waste." Like is too short to waste your talent especially when it can do you some good and make your life a little easier. Don't waste your talent because God has given it to you for positive use.

In addition to trying to find out what your purpose is in life is to look to the people that you admire the most. These types of people can help you do good and make some positive decisions when it comes to changing your life for the better. These people can be your parents, family, friends, or just people that are in the entertainment industry. Everyone has a different life journey to achieve. One of the people that I admire the most would be my mother. The reason why I choose my mother is because of her courage and strength that she had for not just me but for all her children. I never recall her telling or condoning anything that would be wrong. She was a straight up no nonsense type of person and would tell you the truth about yourself rather you wanted to hear it or not.

Another person that I look up to and admire is my uncle John. The reason why I admire him so much is because he was really the same way my mom was. I remember years ago that I was going through something, and he gave me some advice that I would never forget, but at the time I didn't understand, nor did I comprehend what he was talking about, but as I have gotten older, I began to understand. My uncle John always prayed for me and my family before he went back home. He also gave me some words of wisdom that really helped change my way of thinking.

I also admire some of the people that turn their lives around when they overcame adversity to achieve their goals. Some people struggle worse than others. You can never dig a hole so deep that you cannot climb out and be victorious. If you have faith in God and doing his good will, you can make it through anything that you set your mind to. It is just like a song that I was listening to a few years ago and it is called I WROTE MY WAY OUT.

Adversity can be a challenge to overcome especially when you have negative energy and people around you that be doubting you. Sometimes, when you get told so many times that you can't do something or will not secede, you start to believe it and your mindset can put you in a dark place if you let it. That is why it is important to look up to the positive people that you admire and take some of the things that they may say or do into consideration. At the end of the day for your life to change, you are the only one that can make that happen. One of the other tools that you may want to use that involves trying to find your purpose is to volunteer for things.

Volunteering can be one of the most crucial things to use to change your life. I used to hate when my mother would volunteer me for things when I was younger, but at the same time in hindsight I thank her for it.

I was one of the quiet guys when I was

growing up however, when I got older, I learned how and when to use my words wisely. Some people don't try to think things through before speaking and that is how chaos can get started among people.

When you volunteer and work with others to achieve a common goal, your actions can and sometimes pay off for you in the long run. You must think things through before getting into something. Try to have that mindset and optimistic trust that things will work out for you.

CHAPTER

5

NEVER LIMIT YOURSELF

One thing that we must learn in life is NEVER

put a limit on yourself on what you can do. We all

have certain doubts about things that we may say

or do. If you put a limit on yourself, there is a

possibility that you will miss out on the good things

that life has to offer. In personal situations that I

was in, I had to learn an important lesson the hard

way. We can get in our own way when it comes to

changing our lives for the better. God would never

put us in situations that we could not handle. God

will push us to the limit by putting us to the test

each day just to see how far you are willing to go to

follow and do his good will. We all have our

stumbling blocks each day and we all fall short of

God's glory.

Holding on to the belief that anything is

possible is one of the most important things to do

when trying to make that big move in life. You are

going to have your trials and hardships that might

set you back. Them minor setbacks can trigger a

major comeback when you have that positive

mindset and learning not to limit yourself. There

are many outside influences that can cause you to

limit yourself; they can come from family, friends,

or just certain setbacks that you may feel like you

can't get yourself out of. Like I said before, no hole is not too deep to get out of especially when you have God on your side and putting him first in everything in your life. I recall reading the book of Job and it was God that was testing him the whole time, and a woman told him that he should curse God and die, but Job's faith in God was so strong that he told her that she talks like a foolish woman.

Anything is possible when you keep your faith that the job that you want done will get done. I remember when I was in my teens that we were low on food in the house. My mom sent me to the mailbox and there was a check in there, so my mom opened it up and it was for around $3.00. When she looked at it, she told me that it was better than nothing. A few minutes later my brother came in and looked at the check and he told mom

that it was for $300.00, and mom said God is good

and we went out and bought groceries. One of the

most amazing things that came out of that story

was that my mother was grateful with just the

$3.00. Sometimes when you ask God for something

he gives you what you want and then some.

Never giving up can be a challenge, because

sometimes our flesh can become weak and cause

us to throw in the towel so to speak. There were

times that I wanted to give up on life, but I

remembered what my mother would say to me,

"Son you are going to have your tough times, but it

is how you keep your faith by having trust in God

that he will get the job done, do your best and let

God do the rest." I think of my mom daily and miss her with each day that passes me by.

When you are feeling like all is lost, you must find that inner strength to keep going. If you never give up and keep your faith God will come through in the most amazing and awesome way possible. You can be down to your last dollar and God will do something awesome.

I sometimes witness people giving away their last dollar to someone that apparently needed it more than they did. I also witness my own mother doing that for each of her children, when I think about how she used to do that it starts bringing tears to my eyes sometimes. It was nothing but love behind it because she did it with a smile on her face. The things that I reminisce on when I was a child made me want to make some urgent positive changes to my life. My faith has become stronger in God, but there is still work to be done to get where I need and want to be in my life personally.

God has many ways to get our attention. The reason why I say this is because when you are going through a lot in your life sometimes God can cause you to either have a dream/vision or test you by having bad stuff happen that you wouldn't expect.

The soul survivors try to turn their situation into something positive the best way they can. The reason why it's important to never limit yourself when it comes to making them better changes to your life is because sometimes fear and overthinking can hinder us from receiving our blessing from God.

Believing that you are good enough can also be one of the tools to not limit yourself. I used to doubt myself a lot when I was younger, however I had mom and so many father figures in my life to keep going and never give up. The people that were in my corner during the time I was growing up helped me realize that hard work and dedication can pay off when you set your mind on doing something positive with your life.

CHAPTER

6

HAVING FAITH IN GOD

Having faith in God is the most important

thing that we must have for us to succeed in life no

matter what you are trying to do positive. I recall

getting told that I would never get a girlfriend

because I am too nice and don't have that thuggish

attitude. I admit it kind of got to me a little bit but at

the same time I laughed it off because there's a

reason why God got me waiting and I am not

worried about what anyone says or thinks because

I know what I bring to the table and my time and

season is coming. She not only made that statement to me once, but she also said it twice and it really made me angry when she said it.

The aftermath/fall out of the whole thing was that she said we were beefing and to be honest I don't care if this person speaks to me again. She was the one that belittled me and had the nerve to get mad because I put it on social media about what she said to me; I mean first it was an insult and second, she doesn't really know me to say something like that to me in the first place. Despite all this, I will continue to keep my faith in God that something positive will happen in my life. The number one thing that I hate is when they call a good person crazy for getting out of character when they're angry especially when that good person is provoke or being took there. Some people will try to manipulate you and turn it around on you like the situation is your fault but all the while it's theirs. Trust me I am not perfect, but anybody can attest to that I treat people how I want to be treated, I mean that was the way that I was taught, and it is also the golden rule.

There are moments that we may fall weak, but adversity is part of life. Sometimes, I questioned God myself. It is easy to say that you have faith in God when things are going good for us all the time, however the testing comes when things start to get out of our control. God will put us in positions to test our faith and belief that he will get the job done. I have personally seen some people that their lives may not be going too well, but they always manage to keep a smile on their face because they know that God will get them out of the current challenging situation that they may be in. God can change your life; we must trust him.

As for myself I need God each day of my life I mean we all do. I thank God for letting me have another chance to serve him each day that I wake up. Some people do not get the chance to see the next day for many reasons, that's why I feel like that it is a must for me to make the most of each day by being a better person to people and have the confidence to believe in God as well as myself that he will get the job done. Having faith that God will guide you and get the job done is the most crucial thing that you must have for you to make positive changes in your life. Sometimes, when you ask God for one thing, he give you that and then some. God knows all things as well as our thoughts and the things that we are trying to do to change our lives. He also gives us mercy and pardon. There are times that we must reevaluate ourselves as human beings on how we do and say things. We often ask ourselves do we truly have the faith that God will be with us and never leave our side. Christians fall short of God's glory as well as sinners I mean no one is perfect but Jesus Christ himself. Some people are so quick to call people that follow God hypocrites when they mess up, again I say this nobody's perfect. I am far from where I need to be, however each day is a working progress.

CHAPTER

7

LEARNING HOW TO DEAL WITH CHANGE

Some people can handle change, some have a hard time adjusting to it rather it's a physical or mental thing. You may have heard the old saying that for you to get something you never have you must do something you never done; I am a firm believer in that statement. When making them positive changes to your life you will either lose some friends or miss out on temporary fun. I feel that we must set them boundaries for this positive change to take place. The world is changing, and we must change with it. I had to learn how to deal with change myself when I was younger.

One of the best ways to deal with change is by counting your blessings. You might not have the things that you may need or want, but the situation could be so much worse, for example we could be in a foreign country with no running water, food, or just be living in a place where there is dictatorship and no democracy. We as Americans sometimes tend to take little things for granted because we are considered as the greatest country in the world. That is why we should count our blessings and stop complaining about certain things that are irrelevant.

Another example that I will be using as far as

counting your blessings is concerned can relate to prison life. As for me personally I have never gone to prison nor have gotten into any trouble with the law, but I have watched my share of documentaries and heard stories that deterred me from a life of crime. A life of crime will lead to nothing but a dead end. I never wanted to be told when to eat, sleep, shower, or get up by another person. That is why I think about the freedoms that I enjoy daily as far as getting up when I want to or just going somewhere without being restrained. It is the little things that matter to me.

Counting your blessings is a good thing to sit back and think about because there are some people that are less fortunate than we are especially when you go overseas to some of the poorest countries in the world. Never make fun of someone's unfortunate situation because it could be you in a similar situation one day. Life can be a challenge, but it is how we get through it and prevail. I have seen people that were at rock bottom that made the necessary changes to their lives for it to be better. You can have all the money in the world and not be happy. Sometimes, we as people would never know what a person is going through because they would be the ones that are smiling all the time and in good spirits. Just because a person smiles all the time doesn't mean that their life is great. Some people smile and laugh a lot because they feel like that it's the only way to cope with the challenges that life be throwing at us. My late grandfather would always say that you owe anyone the time of day because you never know that it may be all that a person needs to get their spirits up.

For us to adjust to change, we must learn how to create some comfort. One way to make sure that you know how to deal with change would be to make a list of things/hobbies that you like to do to keep yourself busy. When you are creating some comfort in your life, it can make it a little bit better. I never would want to be stuff doing the same thing day after day for the rest of my life. That is why we sometimes need to change some of our routine when we get up in the morning and start our day. Doing the same thing day after day can take a toll on you after a long period of time doing it.

Another thing you can to that will help you cope with change is relax and take a walk by yourself and think things through. Thinking things through can help you be more persist with your decisions that you will have to make in the future. Taking long walks can also calm you down. I honestly think that when taking long walks that they can clear your head with the bad thoughts and doubt that may be going through your head. I remember when my mother and I would have disagreements about things and I would just calm down, give her space, and take a walk and try to figure out things that we can do to resolve the issues that we didn't necessarily agree on all the time. I also remember how we would walk at nighttime and just talk about certain things that either bothered us or just made us happy; I mean I guess I was one of those kids that could talk to my mother about anything that was bothering me, and it was the same, likewise.

When we start to prepare for change, we must also learn how to plan ahead. Planning ahead can be a great tool to use when you trying to either change your life or just learning how to deal with change. When trying to make them positive changes, we must learn to accept any outcome that comes out of the positive change. As we get older and wiser, we must learn how to evolve for us to not get left behind. Change can be hard sometimes, but it is just something we must learn how to adapt to.

Planning things and putting them changes into action can be a hard thing to do. It might not go your way the first time out, however persistence pays dividends. I personally think that I inherit that work ethic from both of my parents because they were both hard working people. You cannot be trying to play around when you are trying to make the positive changes to your life because life is short and our time on this Earth is so little. We must try to get it right while we have the time and the resources. It is just like when you try to tell a child or either a young adult to save money and they feel like that they can spend it but after the money is all gone, they are begging their parents for what they need.

One of the last things that I will be talking about in this chapter when it comes to dealing with change would be to pray a little more. Sometimes, God will not answer your prayers on your time, but he is always on time. As I get older, I have learned how to be more patient when it comes to either waiting on things or just praying and asking God to take care of issues that I personally be dealing with. Pray with some confidence that God will get the job done. NEVER have doubt in your mind wind being on your knees praying to God. Sometimes when things don't go my way, I often think that maybe God didn't want that to happen for me. Everyone has their season when it comes to change and having things go our way.

CHAPTER

8

KNOWING WHEN TO CHANGE

For us to make that big positive change in our lives, we must know when and how to make the move. Some people will try to make the attempt as soon as something negative happens in their lives as for others it may take a little longer to make that big change. I am going to use a drug addict for example, they be doing things that they would not normally do to get their next fix, however after they acquired it and the high wears off then they are still stuck with the same problems that they are trying to escape from. Sooner or later a change will need to be made.

Another example that I will use will have something to do with a person that goes to work every day and not like his or her job at all. It doesn't necessarily be the job itself; it be the people that are running it. I always said that when you are unhappy with your daily routine as far as getting up going to work and coming home frustrated about your job, you do not feel like you're living your best life at all just existing. It doesn't have to be just about the money you are being paid it could be more to the fact that you're not happy with your job. In some cases, it can be more to a person not being happy with their job than meets the eye. Some people will try to find a balance between their job and home life for them to stay happy. All the money in the world don't mean anything if you're not happy. I have heard about people with a lot of money commit suicide just because of not being happy with their current lifestyle, and I am a firm believer that the more money you have the more problems will come with it.

It is up to us to take that big step to that positive change; it doesn't happen overnight. I know that I keep saying things about my mother in this book, but she was a wise woman that told the truth to your face rather you wanted to hear it or not. It takes some people longer than others to realize that a change needs to be made. We can either change our lives in a positive way to have the lifestyle that we may want, or we can stay in the same rut and be angry and miserable all the time. I never really want to be around people that are just miserable and not thankful for anything that God has blessed them. You can give a person the whole world and they still will not be satisfied.

For us to know when to change, we must learn not to live in the past. Leave the past where it is because at the end of the day it will hold you back from getting your blessings from God when you dwell on it for too long. I have had personal experiences on holding onto the past when all It was doing to me was making me miserable and angry all the time. Letting go the past can be a tall order especially when you are the one that had been wronged in a certain way. I sometimes have a history of holding grudges against certain people, but I had to come to the realization that I had to let them go and move on. Sometimes, the best revenge is none because it can hinder you from either moving on or receiving your blessings from God. I also had to learn that the people that mistreated me for no reason will have to face God for that, and I said to myself from now on I am letting the Lord fight my battles for me.

Another thing on when to know when to change is to realize that the old way of doing things has run its course. The reason I say that is because sooner or later you will get tired of repeating the same behavior or cycle all the time. Before I got a job, I was just getting up walking around my neighborhood every day. I woke up one morning and decided that enough is enough, I was almost in a depression because I had friends that had cars, their own place, and making money and all I was doing was either playing video games or just walking around my neighborhood day after day. It was not that I wasn't willing to work, it was more so trying to find a job in my area. It was a frustrating time for me especially when I just graduated from college, and I wasn't getting any calls back for the jobs that I had applied for at the time. Even though sometimes I may not like my job, nevertheless I am glad God blessed me with one. The things that we may say or do can and will get old after a while. That is why knowing when to change at the right time is a good thing. It is just like that old saying to much of a good thing can also be bad in the long run.

It is just like working at a job that don't want to let you have hardly any days off; of course, the money is good but what is the use of it when you don't have any time to spend it much less enjoy it. In recent years I reminisce on times when I said I wish that I was an adult, but now I understand when parents tell us to stay a kid for as long as you can and never rush your time, everyone and everything has its season under the sun. Life is too short to either be dwelling on the past or either being afraid and knowing to make that positive change and realize enough is enough.

CHAPTER

9

GOING AFTER THE LIFE YOU WANT

When trying to go after the life you want you are going to encounter some adversity, challenges, and temptation. Adversity is a part of life. Adversity is personally one of my favorite words to use when describing life's challenges. Some people struggle worse than others in life, but it is how your mindset and willingness to make that change to get out the bad situation that you are currently in. One of the reasons why the word adversity is one of my favorite words to use is because when someone tells me that I can't accomplish something that I want to achieve, I try my best to prove them wrong

that it is possible that the goals that I want to

achieve can be done. Going after the life you want

will not be a walk in the park. I was always taught

that for you to get what you want out of life, you

had to work hard for it. I just don't want to just do

enough to get by. Some of the athletes that we

have the privilege to watch on TV had to work hard

to get where they wanted to be in life; I really think

that's what separates the good players from the

great ones. The great ones are never comfortable

with just being good enough to make it to the big

time so to speak. You will have your days that you

will want to just give up however, it is just the fight

and the persistence that may keep you going. Like I

said in the last chapter you must know when to

change and hope for the best. There are days that I don't be feeling like going to work, but I know that I must make a living for myself and pray that it will be a good day.

Never give up on what you may want to accomplish in life just because some people don't want to see you win or have doubt in you. It is just like some people think that I won't get into a relationship because I am too nice; I admit it gets to me, but God is in control and there are reasons why it is not my season yet. There is a time and place for everything. I haven't given up, that is what the devil wants me to do.

I always told myself that I wanted to buy a house when I was younger. I knew that it would take a lot of hard work to make it happen, but I've

kept my faith in God, and I also did my part and

waited for the time to be right. I had that goal set

since I was a little kid; I didn't know how I was

going to make it happen, but I remained steadfast

in my goal and made it possible. I decided a long

time ago that I wasn't going to live in an apartment

for the rest of my life. You only live once and life is

very short. I was taught the value of hard work at a

young age. I wouldn't say that I was completely

shelter as a child, but my mother would tell me as

well as warn me about certain things that I would

have to encounter for me to achieve my goals. She

also taught me how to work and earn the privileges

and the stuff I may want out of life and to this day

the philosophy is and will always be instilled in me

for the rest of my life.

Nobody is going to give you the life you want to have. Getting out and earning your own living is a must. When you go out and earn your living, I mean it can be from just buying your first car to just getting an apartment, you tend to appreciate it more and do your best to keep it verses things that were always given to you.

For us to go after the life we may want, you will have to make some changes to your life. You will have to be willing to evolve with the time because things are starting to get more advanced as time goes on. The first things that needs to be changed is our mindset on things. Being more optimistic will help you get through the changing process in life. We must learn to look at the bigger and better picture when looking and thinking about certain situations. Got to limit or eliminate any kind of doubt or discouragement that we may have in our minds. You also must try to stay away from people that are simple minded and don't see the good in you because overtime they will hinder you from going after the life you may want. It took me some years to learn how to get rid of the doubt and just do my best in what I want to achieve in life. I am still a student of trying to get rid of some doubt and discouragement I may have in my mind.

Always try to follow your gut feeling when going after the life you may want because most of the time when it's too good to be true, most of the time it really is. You also must watch out for the people who will try to sell you false dreams when trying to change your life. Some people that are not doing anything positive with their own lives will try their best to bring you down on their level where you do not need to be.

One of the most important things you must have when it comes to going after the life you want is consistency. The words consistency and dedication both go hand in hand because when you are trying hard to achieve a certain goal, you may start to get that mentality about not taking the word no for an answer when it comes to making certain changes to your life. Try not to have the negative thoughts in your mind when it comes to life changes.

The definition of the word consistent is acting or done in the same way over time, especially to be fair or accurate. Consistency can be something simple as coming to work on time every day and never being late. I was always taught to show up on time for any kind of an appointment so I wouldn't get that label as being a person that is late all the time or never shows up when he or she said they would. People will look and see how consistent you are because it can be a major asset to them as well as yourself. When going after the life you may want consistency must play an important role in your progress. Consistency can be a challenge when you either don't have the funds or the resources to go after the life you want.

CHAPTER
10
BETTERING YOURSELF

When we talk about making good changes to our lives bettering yourself comes up in the conversation. It is a process and doesn't happen overnight. We must have that never give up or never give in mentality for these life changes to happen. You may have heard the old saying that actions speak louder than words, and to be honest this is a very true statement. You can say that you are going to make good on a promise that you either made to yourself or to someone else, but when your actions do not match up with your promise, your words do not mean anything to anyone.

I was always taught to be a man of my word. When I say that I am going to do something for someone nine times out of ten it gets done unless something comes up and I cannot deliver on the word that I gave to that person. We are only human; we are not going to deliver all the time on our word. The thing that I personally have a problem with when people talk about keeping their word is that when it is time to get the job done, they will try to beat around the bush and give you the run around on why they cannot do something that they said that they were going to do. I understand if something comes up, but when you are just wasting someone's time when you are still telling them that you are going to do something for them, but all the while you never were going to do it, then that makes people trust you even less. In my honest opinion keeping your word is one of the most important parts of bettering yourself.

We must learn to make sacrifices when trying to make positive things happen in our lives. Do not choose temporary fun over trying to better yourself in life. Even when we are trying to serve God daily, we must learn to make unpopular decisions that other people may not agree with. God must be involved for us to better ourselves in life.

One of the ways to better yourself is to get active. Being active can put you in good spirits and lift hope. When getting active, we must learn how to step out our comfort zone occasionally. Ever since I been working at my job, I have been socializing a little bit more in each of the years I have been there. My mother used to say to me all the time that nothing ventured nothing gained; what she meant by that statement is that if I didn't go out into the world and mingle with people that I would be stuck in the same rut for a long period of time. I was not really a people person, but as I have gotten older, that was starting to change in my life. I even like to play pickup basketball games with people from time to time. I am not saying that we should go out every weekend; I am simply saying that when you stay active and outgoing the more friends and positive people you attract. Life is too short to stay in the same rut and not explore life and what it has to offer in a positive way, it is just like Jesus told a parable in the Bible about the men with the talents.

Having compassion for other is another way to better yourself. I admit in my early 20s I didn't always agree on having compassion for certain people because they use their sad story to manipulate you when they are talking about their dilemma that they may be going through. I have learned how to have compassion for others as I have gotten older because I learn that when you are on your feet go and help someone else when they are struggling and have an open heart and mind when talking to them. When I have got older, I was beginning to understand why my mother did the things that she did for people. I hope that one day that I will be as nice and courageous as she was during the time that she was with us.

Another way that we can learn how to better

ourselves during the changing process is by eliminating recurring habits. Recurring habits can be anything from not looking a person in the eye when talking to them to just not choosing the right words to say in certain situations. I sometimes still have the habit of not looking a person in the eye from time to time. I really feel that eye contact is important especially trying to apply for a job that you may want. I am good at looking a person in the eye because they are human just like I am and deserve the respect that I would want myself. When you don't look a person in the eye, most of the time they're not going to take you serious at all. I learned from a long time ago that I had to be brave and not fear simple things like that. Well, I guess the habit kelp happening because I would use it as a defense mechanism so to speak. I really have gotten a lot better at looking a person in the eye as I have gotten older.

Another habit that I will be talking about is word choosing. I always was told that I talk so proper, and I take that as a compliment. I guess I inherit that trait from my father. As I have gotten older, every time I hear a word that I have never heard before I look up the meaning of it and try to use it in a conversation when I am talking to people. Expanding your vocabulary is one of the many ways to better yourself in life. There is nothing wrong with either learning something new every day or just improving your vocabulary on how to use certain words in different situations in life. Sometimes, it's not what you say it is how you say it; what I mean by that would be the tone of voice that you may be using at the time. You can say some of the nicest things to people, however it your tone does not parallel to what you are saying then most of the time it doesn't mean anything to the person that you may be having a conversation with. I always try my best to talk in a tone that does not hurt people feelings because one thing that I have that cannot be taken away from me is compassion for people's feelings. Like I said before if I hurt someone unintentionally then I will apologize for my actions. Bettering yourself in life by getting rid of the habits that I just talked about is a must if you want to be a big success.

The final way that I will be talking about as far

as bettering yourself is to eat healthy and hydrate daily. I recall the times when I was little that I was a picky eater. I wouldn't eat certain foods that mom or some of my family members prepared for us; over the years as I got older, I started to come around and eat a little bit healthier. A healthy eating habit can make you feel great mentally as well as physically. I never had a drink of alcohol in my life and for most of the people that I tell that to is hard to believe. I have been tempted before but remained steadfast. The point that I am trying to make is that when you drink too much alcohol the side effects will catch up to you in the long run. I'm not trying to deter anyone from alcohol by any means, but when you have too much of a good thing then you will get burned out on it.

CHAPTER

11

ENCOURAGING OTHERS IN A POSITIVE WAY

I was always taught that if you are on your feet and able to help somebody else while they are going through a hard time in life. Not only it's the right thing to do, but it is also what God expects us to do when others are in need. No one is above anybody; we all go through things rather good or bad. Life is already hard enough to be belittling people that are less fortunate or don't have anything. Some people are just selfish when it comes to either helping people or just not wanting to help anyone at all.

You may be asking yourself how this helps you with positive changes in your life; well, I am going to explain. Positive changes to your life have a lot to do with helping others that are in need. It is a great feeling to help other people when they are either feeling inferior about themselves or just down on their luck. There have been times that I have been in certain situation that I would feel down or sorry for myself when I am alone in my house, but the thing that I do is read my bible in pick myself back up and say to myself that God will handle anything that I am going through. Encouraging others in a positive way can go a long way in their lives as well as yours. My mother used to say to us that charity begins at home and spreads abroad.

One of the ways that we can help encourage

others is by not talking down to them when they either mess up or don't know any better. When you talk down to a person that is trying to do right, you are nothing more than part of the problem. Be a part of the solution not the problem.

Talking down to or about a person to make yourself look good is one of the lowest things to do; I personally have been guilty of it from time to time. Help that person to make them necessary changes to their life so that they can achieve their goals that life has to offer. Never kick a person while they're down because the same way God gave you certain things, he also can take it away from you.

Remember this statement and never forget it; how a person treats you rather good or bad is how they really feel about you.

I had an ex-girlfriend from a long time ago that treated me so bad but looking back now it taught me that anyone can switch up on you and you didn't have to do anything to them for it to happen. She did not care about me the way I cared for her, and it took me years to realize that.

If you a going to talk and belittle someone just because they are less fortunate, at least try to help them out by either being there for them or just doing good deeds for them, however if you are not going to do those things that I just talked about then shut the hell up about them because you are nothing more than part of the problem not the solution.

In addition to helping people is to never count favors. Jesus said in the bible that do good for people and expect nothing back because we will have a great reward in Heaven.

I am a firm believer in that statement. It is just like a couple that or either just in a relationship or married, it is a team thing that you both work on every day. I have brothers and sisters that I would help if they needed me and would not expect anything from them in return. When making them life changes, you must think about other people to that got you where you are or trying to get you where you need to be in life.

CHAPTER
12

TAKING RESPONSIBILITY FOR YOUR ACTIONS

When making them positive changes to your life one of the first things that we must learn to do is take responsibility for our own actions. We all make mistakes but taking responsibility for them can be a tall order sometimes. We tend to blame others for either the way we act or just the things that we do. I learned a long time ago that if you either wronged or hurt someone in any way to apologize for it. Some people think that they are never wrong and don't have to do it. There are also some people let pride get in the way when they know that they are wrong and play victim during the ordeal; I personally call people like that narcissist.

I honestly feel like if you are not where you want to be in life, you shouldn't go around either blaming other people or being mad at yourself. You must want to make the changes in your life and be persistent about it. I am going to use an example involving the cops. Let's just say for instants that you may be doing something that is illegal, and someone reports it to the police; you can't get mad when you get in trouble and get hauled off to jail because at the end of the day it is your fault. We all make mistakes; you start to become an adult when you own up to them and try to rectify and fix them.

There are people that are my age that will never admit when they are in the wrong either because of their ego or their pride gets in the way. You really start to make them positive steps when you try to fix your mistakes that you may have made in life.

Sometimes in life it is better to be at peace than it is to be right all the time. My mother would tell me that if I was right about something stand on it, don't argue with people that don't have an open mind about things that are quick to jump to conclusions without getting the facts first about certain people or situations. It took me some years to realize that you don't get anywhere arguing with a person that is simple minded. It takes a lot of growing up and outgrowing things to make them good changes to your life. One of the best ways to do good in life is by having that positive mindset. Some people do have problems when admitting fault because they feel like they are never wrong. Being teachable when it comes to life changes when you are wrong can be another sign of growing up and being an adult. There are people that are my age that throw a fit like a child when things don't go their way or being told no all the time, and I be like will this person ever grow up and be an adult. I am guilty of it from time to time especially when it comes to working in a factory. I'm not saying that you shouldn't complain about certain situations in life, however when you do it daily it starts to feel like nothing will satisfy this person no matter what you do for them. No matter what you may do for people they're never happy.

CHAPTER
13
CREATE A POSITIVE ROUTINE

In my opinion I really think that for you to get out the negative rut that you may be in is to get a good routine going. Having hobbies can be a part of the positive change that you may want to make in your life. Everyone may have a different way to start their day as soon as they wake up; they either get in the shower first then eat breakfast or they may have taken their shower the night before. The point that I am trying to make is that everybody has their own way of doing things in the morning when they wake up. My personal routine every night is before I go to bed, I read a few verses in my bible to give me peace of mind and pray afterwards. We must learn to give God some of our time no matter what, because that is what he wants and expects from us. When you have that positive routine going, the chances of you having a good day goes up high. I would love to have a great day every day, but life doesn't always work out the way you plan or want it to be. One thing that I learned from my mother is that don't let anyone, or anything ruin your day.

Like I said before, you cannot be around negative and miserable people and expect to make progress in your life. Negative people will try to bring you down just because they're unhappy with their lives. I used to let small things get to me when I was younger, but I learned that people are going to be people and stay away from negative energy. It's alright to talk to everyone, but we must learn to distant ourselves from the bad influences that may try to bring us down. One of the ways to get a positive routine going is by laying out plans for what you want to do with your life. Some people are just living in the moment and hoping for the best and expecting the worse to come and that's no way to be living life. If we expect the worse all the time, we would be miserable. I can honestly say that I had a plan when I was eleven years old that consisted of going to college and becoming a professional basketball player. In my opinion, if you don't have a dream of becoming something positive then why wake up and just live in the moment sad and miserable all the time. Laying out plans for your future can give you at least a sense of direction on where to go. I may not have become a ball player, but I did accomplish one of my other goals by going to college and graduating with an associate degree in business administration. I have seen little kids as young as ten years old have more goals and ambition than some adults and that's a shame in my opinion. You must have the right people in your corner to make them changes in your life for the better.

Being consistent with trying to change your life is essential. Consistency is the key to them life changes that you may want to make. I cannot stress enough about consistency because you can't do certain things when you are not putting your best effort into it. It is just like when you are talking to a person that you may want a relationship with one day; I mean the feelings are mutual and everything, but the consistency isn't there. The reason why I say this is because rather you really like or have feelings for someone, you are going to make time for them in some of the best ways you can and vice versa. I much rather deal with a clingy person than a person that takes days to answer just one text message. The feelings for both parties can be mutual and everything, however if one party is putting in all the effort in the potential relationship, then maybe it may be time to makes some changes in your life even if it hurts.

Tracking your progress can be another way to create a positive routine. I'm not saying that you should track it 24/7, just every so often. The progress that you may be making as far as changing your life can take some time; I mean it doesn't happen overnight. I am still a working progress myself because I feel like that I am not where I want to be at in my life currently. If you are felling inferior, try your best to make yourself superior. I always lived by this principle by saying to myself do your best and let God do the rest. Another example that I am going to use is working out and losing weight. When we go to the gym, we all expect instant results as soon as our workout is done, however you don't lose weight overnight, that's where the word consistency comes into play. Whatever you want in life you must work for it and be always persistent.

CHAPTER

14

SET REALISTIC GOALS

When it comes to them life changes, one of
the main things that you must acquire is a clear
mindset about the things that you may want to do.
A positive mindset is important to have because
your mind must be clear from all the things that
may distract you throughout the process of
changing your life. Each day that we wake up we
have another chance to get our lives going in the
right direction. You are going to have your ups and
downs throughout life; however, it is how you
handle and endure the situations that comes our
way.

When setting goals, you must try to figure out what your goals are in life. It is obvious that you may want to make them changes to your life for the better, but you must have a gameplan/strategy on how you are going to go about doing just that. You must have that get up and go about yourself for you to make your dreams come true. I recall a time when I kept saying to myself that I want to own a house one day. I also remember that for me to make this happen I had to make sacrifices. Now I own a car and paying a mortgage on a house because I set them goals at a young age and was very persistent in my journey to make these two things happen, and it was also a life changing event for me. I remain humble to this day because I never know what may happen to me; in my opinion that is the mysterious thing about life it can be unpredictable sometimes.

Also, when you are setting goals in life the word discipline will come into play. You may want to go out to eat with some of your friends but at the same time you may be trying to save up for something special; that is when the word sacrifice comes into play as well because a few hours of fun eventually wear off when you don't have a dime to your name because you may have spent most of your money just for a moment of pleasure. I am not saying that we can't have a good time and enjoy friends, but we must know our limits when it comes to spending money and how much that ties in to making your life changes come into reality.

One of the main things to have when it comes to setting goals is to stay confident that all things will work out. I'm not going to say that I had a confidence problem, but I was an overthinker. Overthinking in my opinion is not a healthy thing to do at all. I often catch myself overthinking and stressing about certain situations that I have no control over. Overthinking can also cause you to have sleepless nights as well. I had to learn to leave things in God's hands because stressing about things that we have no control over can damage your mind in a phycological way. Over the years I had to learn to be more confident and trust in God a lot more because in these last days of time we need him now more than ever before because the devil is busy and will do what he must do to acquire your soul. Every day we wake up our souls are at stake.

Do not let anyone or anything come between your goals in life. Life is too short to not have a dream that you may make it out your current situation one day. I learned a long time ago to keep my faith because at the end of the day God is in control. When a certain goal feels like that it is unreachable, you may just want to give up and go back to your old way of doing things by staying in the same rut. I also learned in life that there are certain roads that you may have to take alone with just you and God and let him guide you through adversity. We must find that inner strength that we need to keep pushing towards our goals and learn to be relentless.

There are some people that like their solitude a lot and I am one of them. There is nothing wrong with being alone in my opinion. Sometimes, when you step out of your comfort zone, it can be the best thing you could ever do for yourself. We must learn to be relentless and don't let anyone put a ceiling on anything that we may want to accomplish in life. It is just like a person applying for a job for the first time; he or she really wants to work but they have not heard anything back from the job. They may be asking themselves what they do wrong I mean they have no criminal record and are well qualified for the job; these are questions they are asking themselves. To be honest there is an untold/unwritten secret when it comes to applying for a job in some cases; if you really want the job that bad you stay on them, be relentless, and have that positive attitude when you go in for the interview for it. You can't just fill out an application and not do anything afterwards; you must show the place of employment that you really want the job more than anyone else and put the work ethic into it when you get it.

The last thing that I will be talking about in this chapter is being sure about what you can do in life. You may have heard the saying that America is the land of opportunity, but for you to make your goals a reality you must be sure and positive about what you want to do in life. There are millions of people every day that come to America to make something positive of themselves; that is why I am proud to be an American.

CHAPTER
15
STAYING AWAY FROM NEGATIVITY

Staying away from negativity might be one of the most essential things we must do for us to making them important changes to our lives. I remember when I was playing basketball in junior high school when I was a kid; one game I did not score a single point, but I was a standout on defense, people were coming up to me saying that I couldn't score, and it got me down a little bit. When people had their negative comments, I did my best to tune them out because it would have hindered me in the long run. The point that I am trying to make is people or going to be people and you cannot stop them from talking about you rather it is good or bad.

The more adversity that you deal with the stronger and relentless you become. Some people relish on the fact that they are going to face adversity in life when it comes to positive change because they know in the back of their minds that persistence pays off and God rewards people that are trying their best to change their life in a positive way. Doing the right thing is not always easy. Sometimes, you must swallow your pride for you to achieve your goals. The average person in that may be in high school starts working part time until they are able to get in the position to be in a better situation. After I graduated in the year 2008,

I worked part time in a grocery store until I got into college. I didn't care about what people may have thought of me during that point because I knew that I was going to be in a better situation.

You may have heard that old saying that goes like this, *"God is going to bless you so make preparations for it."* I am a firm believer in that saying. We must have faith and patients when it comes to waiting on God. Do not get jealous of others because they are getting their blessing faster than you are because it is their season and God has the time and the season for you to have what you asked for. Everyone had their own time in season for everything.

Another way to try to keep the negativity to a

minimum is to stay away from the bad influences. When certain people observe, you are trying to change your life they may be happy for you one the outside but envy from within. When it comes to the people that want you to fail, it is more to them than meets the eye. Also, when people are doubting you behind your back, they were never your friends to begin with. The smaller circle you have when it comes to people the better off you are; as for me I guess I like my solitude too much sometimes, I mean even when I was a kid, I was shy and did not really play with the other kids when I was in kindergarten. I am not saying that we should alienate everyone and be by ourselves, however the point that I am trying to get across is we need to keep that negativity to a minimum.

Setting boundaries when dealing with negativity is a must when it comes to achieving goals in life. I learned to try my best to avoid arguing with someone when I know that I am in the right because it is just like me arguing with a stop sign. It takes two to argue and debate on certain things. I recall the time that I was talking to this female about a potential relationship with each other; I honestly believe that we wouldn't mess with each other for the simple fact that we debated on things instead of talking about them like adults. I would be ignored when I was trying to be the adult about things. She also had to nerve to not speak to me for a while because she wanted so called peace, however you can't say that you want peace and be the cause of the chaos at the same time, I mean how the hell does that work; Dr Phil would have a hard time figuring this one out in my opinion.

I also find it funny when someone is mistreating you for no reason at all and try to put the blame on you by calling you crazy because they got called out on their BS. The thing with me is that I will not beg anyone to get a conversation out of them at all. The way a person treats you is how they really fill about you rather it's good or bad. It is just like the time I put a statement that a girl made about me that was negative to my face twice on social media about how I would never get a girlfriend; I mean she was the one that said it and insulted me twice to my face, I mean she doesn't know me for real so who the heck is she to judge me.

The point that I am making is that you do not have to tolerate people disrespecting you for no reason especially when they do not know anything about you. Setting boundaries when it comes to changing your life is a must. Do not disrespect anybody and NEVER allow yourself to be disrespected. We also must learn to forgive the people that mistreat us. I learned how to forgive a long time ago, but that doesn't mean that you let the same people that mistreat or disrespect you for no reason back into your life again so they can do it once more. I have forgiven both people that did me wrong by making them statements against me and glad to be on good terms with them.

CHAPTER

16

PUTTING GOD FIRST IN ANYTHING YOU SET YOUR MIND TO

Trusting God and putting him first is the most

important thing to do when it comes to making

certain changes to your life. It is also important to

give God praise rather things are going good or bad

in your life. God did not say that when you start to

make them positive changes to your life that it was

going to be a walk in the park so to speak. We must

learn to work for what we want and not settle for

less than our best. I recall reading this post on

Facebook and it said something like this would you

rather talk to Jesus or take a billion dollars; my

personal choice would be sitting down and having a conversation with Jesus. I like money but not in love with it, I love God more. God has got me out of some bad and questionable situations in the past. The good lord knows all things; we just need to trust him more and let him take control of our lives especially now more than ever.

It is like I said before, with God all things are possible. I admit that there have been moments that I have gotten weak, but I remained steadfast in my faith that God will work out any situation that I may be dealing with in life. Some people struggle worse than others, but those who are the survivors will do their best to turn something negative in to positive. It is all about the will power that we need to have for us to follow Jesus even when it is hard sometimes. Doing the right thing is not always easy, but it doesn't go unnoticed.

When reading the bible a little bit more can give you some sense of direction when it comes to putting God first when you set your mind on doing something. I will be one of the first ones to admit that when reading the bible, I have a hard time putting it down once I start. The bible is one of them books that you can't just put down when you start reading it from my personal experiences. I will also be one of the first people to admit that I should read the bible more often than I have been in the past. We must know the word of God for us to do his will. We must also have faith in ourselves as well as having it in God. I love God and he will always come first in my life. I thank God each day that I wake up; I say to myself I am not dead, in jail, nor disabled. Giving God the praise in everything that we do in life is a must. I am just thankful that I have friends, family, and my coworkers that really care about me and love me and likewise for them in return. It is a great feeling that God gave his only son to die on the cross for our sins because he loved us so much.

Faith in yourself in all that you are trying to achieve in life is a very important asset to have in life. We all fall short when it comes to obeying God sometimes; that is why it is up to us to ask for forgiveness for our sins. I also believe that God works through other people for us to get the help we may need to succeed in life. Everyone needs somebody for help, so never be too proud or let pride get in the way of that. When we have God in our lives, we can conquer anything that life may throw at us. It is just like a child that depends on their parents to take care of them; that child hardly ever lose faith in their parents especially when it comes to something that is important. If God ever bless me with children, one day I will be the best father that I can be to the best of my ability rather I am with their mother or not.

One other thing that we also need to learn as far as putting God first in our lives is with him all things are possible. Through my time that I have been alive, I have seen God work many wonders when it comes to changing people's lives. When we wake up in the morning, God is giving us another chance to get right with him because tomorrow is not promise. One of the greatest highlights of my life was when I got saved at the age of 15; I am not perfect by any means, but I never forget where I come from or how I was raised. God gives us free will and a choice to follow and obey him. You may think that you are damaged goods or a lost cause so to speak, but all the sudden God comes into your life and makes sure that you are ok and get you back in his favor. Sometimes when you want something or something to happen so bad and it doesn't it may turn out to be a blessing in disguise because God may be preparing you for a better situation in life. With man it is impossible, but with God all things are possible.

The last thing that I will be talking about in this chapter has something to do with giving God more of our time. I will be the first one to say that I haven't been giving the good Lord enough time in my life, but that is about to change. God deserves more of our time. I recently started to read my bible a little bit more each day and pray before going to work. Spending time with God even when your life is going great is also the thing to do; don't just go to him when things are going bad. When we learn to give God control, he can change our lives in a positive way. God also warns us about certain things that will take place when it comes to following him.

Never be ashamed or embarrassed that you follow and obey God. He knows that we are not perfect, but when you are trying to follow God to the best to your ability, it doesn't go unnoticed at all. We serve an awesome God because he gives us mercy and pardon. When your faith is as much as the size of a mustard seed, you can move mountains. Things will start to work out in our favor when we learn to trust God that he will get the job done. One of the things that I remember about my mother is that every time I left the house to go to work, she would always tell me to ask the Lord for favor as I would be walking out the door. Even to this day I can picture her saying it to either me or one of my siblings and that made me feel good and have the faith that everything will work out in my favor.

CHAPTER 17

LEAVING THE PAST WHERE IT IS

Leaving the past where it is or letting things go can be a tall order at times. It is hard for me personally because one of the most frustrating things to happen to me is being mistreated or done wrong knowing that I didn't do anything to deserve it. A lot of people live with hurt and let it fester inside of them so long that it starts to consume them. I started getting on my knees and praying that God take all this anger that I am feeling away from me so I can finally be at peace.

Maintaining your sanity is important when making them life changes for the better. I thank God every day that I have a forgiving heart. I am a strong believer in second chances because we all make mistakes and stumble from time to time. It is just like my ex-girlfriend from a long time ago did me wrong for no reason by disrespecting and embarrassing me in my own neighborhood for no reason at all in front of quite a few people. I forgave her, but for me to keep my sanity I had to leave her alone for good and move on with my life because she was not going to do anything but be a toxic person and that really became apparent in my own neighborhood back in the summer of 2009. It is like I said before, how a person treats you rather it is good or bad is how they really feel about you. I like to also add that what made the situation even worse was she came by my house disturbing my peace just because she didn't know what she wanted, or she may have known what she wanted but felt like she could have her cake and eat it to. Again, I forgave her and moved on with my life.

If we let ourselves become a prisoner of the past, we can't grow or learn from it because it has consumed us. We must be focused on the future by moving forward and leaving the past where it is. I often ask myself when I was going through the things that I was going through because I never wanted to walk around angry about something that went wrong in my past. How will we have a future or maintain the happiness if we keep replaying the past in our mind? Overtime it will make you mentally exhausted as well as lose a sense of who you are.

Well also must learn to give ourselves permission to talk about the past. When you have a good friend to lean on, it means a lot. I wasn't good at talking about what I was feeling with certain people because of the fear of either being made fun of or just simply being ignored. I honestly believe that is why so many people contemplate suicide because they feel like that their feelings do not matter to anyone and many of them are men. I had to learn a long time ago that talking about your feelings can lift a huge burden off your shoulders. I vividly remember the summer of 2009 too well because I felt like that I was in a depression until towards the end of the summer that my mother had my uncle pray for me and give me some advice that sticks with me to this day.

For us to make them big changes in our life, we must think about the future and move forward. With all things considered, I really do enjoy my life because I look forward to another day and try to be a better person than I was the day before. Yesterday is dead and over and we can't get it back. I look forward to seeing my nieces and nephews grow up and be good God-fearing men and women in his eyes.

We also need to prepare for what God has in store for us and we will not be able to do that if we keep holding on to the past. It is just like a person that is getting out of prison for the first time; I have never been to prison, but I have heard and listen to stories on how that they were scared when they got out because they had no sense of direction and that itself can be overwhelming. It is just like Tupac said in a song, *"just because you are from the ghetto doesn't mean you can't grow."* Remember, it is ok to talk about your feelings with someone that you trust even if you are a man. Do not let anyone tell you any different because they have never walked a mile in your shoes, so who are they to judge you. Leave the past where it is and trust God. People will have their opinions and try to paint this horrible picture of you when trying to let the past go and change in a positive way simply because of the fear that you may go further than them. When you have God on your side, the possibilities are limitless.

When it comes to changing your life in a positive way as far as leaving the past where it is you must accept the fact that the person that wronged you may not apologize for their actions. I learned a long time ago that when you are in the wrong, the adult thing to do is to take responsibility for your actions; for some people that can be a challenge because their pride may be on the line. I will never let my pride get in the way because I realize that we are all human and got feelings. Trust me, there are some people that are my age that still act like children from time to time.

I know that I be still bringing up my ex-girlfriend from time to time, and I know for a fact

that she will never apologize to me under any

circumstances; I had to accept that and move on

with my life because if I would sit there and dwell

on it day after day, then I would be in a mental

prison and that would drive me insane. It is ok to

love someone, however, do not lose who you are or

your sanity by trying too hard to please them and

they are not giving you the same gratitude in

return. It is also like when a parent and child have

a disagreement about something; sometimes the

parent will not admit when they are wrong, and the

argument does nothing but escalate so bad that

neither you are your parent are speaking anymore.

I will be that one of the first ones to admit that my

mother and I had disagreements, but we always

saw each other's point of view and worked it out; it never had gotten so bad that we wouldn't speak to each other. I had to realize that I am the child and she was my parent and I sat down and listened; when I was wrong I apologized and vice versa. People make mistakes including parents; I mean we are all human.

CHAPTER

18

PAY MORE ATTENTION TO YOUR LIFE

Sometimes in this game of life when before

we start to make them necessary changes to it, we

must learn to sit down and do a self-evaluation on

ourselves on how it is going. Like I said before

self-evaluation can be a challenge. It is just life if

you were in one relationship after another and

something always goes wrong from disagreements

to just down-right being disrespectful to each

other. Just sit back and think about what you are

doing wrong instead of blaming everyone else all

the time because who knows maybe you are part of

the problem. I have not been in that many

relationships throughout my life, but I have talked to some women and the relationship idea fell through so to speak. I had to figure out what I was doing wrong and started to question myself why because I knew what I brought to the table and that was good intentions; I lived by this philosophy that if my intentions are not good, I will not disturb someone else's peace. Also, I learned another philosophy that if you can't solve a problem you eliminate it especially when you have done your best to rectify the situation.

I often ask myself sometimes am I happy with where I am at in my life. I struggled to come to an understanding that I am not because I honestly feel like I could do more with my life if I can put my mind to it. I believe that sometimes we become too comfortable with our lives when we can do so much better. For us to make this giant leap of faith a reality, we must try our best to get rid of self-doubt. Believe it or not I thought that I would never be a homeowner at the rate I was going a few years ago; then I finally got my big break when I got hold of some money that I would need to make this happen. It was all in God's time that he would make it happen for me, and all I had to do is work hard and keep my faith.

Our faith gets tested daily by God. It is up to us to find that inner strength that we will need to make our goals become a reality. God expects us to do our part as well. God listens to us when we pray; we just must trust him that he will come through in his time.

When doing an evaluation on your life and how it is going, we must have self-awareness about ourselves. One of the things that we can do is to remove the mental blocks that are holding us back from achieving our goals. Anything can hold us back from making them big changes that we need to make for us to be successful. When I was in the process of trying to own a home, I knew that I had challenges that awaited me. I overcame a lot of hurdles that were in my way because I had God on my side and will power that I was going to get this house no matter what I had to go through to get it. I did not let anyone, or anything deter me from doing what I needed to do to make my dream a reality.

CHAPTER

19

DON'T STRESS OVER WHAT YOU CAN'T CONTROL

One of the major things that we must learn when it comes to changing our life in a positive way is to not stress over things we cannot control. At the end of the day, God is in control of every situation; he knows our needs and the things that we may desire to have or want to do. God is always on time; it may not be the time that we want, but nevertheless he will never leave us. When it comes to me personally, I tend to stress over things that I may not have any control over, but as I have gotten older, I try to think things through before I start to put my plan or anything that I want to do into action. I will be the one of the first people to admit that I wasn't always as patient as I am now especially in my early 20s.

Stressing over things that we cannot control will drive you crazy. We must learn to take things slow and a day at a time. Life is too short to be stressing over things we cannot control. One of the other things that I may have inherit from my mother would be that I tend to stress out quite a bit especially in certain life situations. We never know what our parents go through when they are laying down at night worried about either a bill or some food for the house; they may be worried about how they are going to get the money together while us kids are just laying down sleep like we don't have a care in the world, but don't have any idea what our parents go through to get the things we need. I never recalled going to bed hungry as an adolescent.

One of the main traits that we may have when it comes to stressing about certain things in life is overthinking. Overthinking can be one of the things that can make you go crazy because when it happens it can mess you up in a phycological way. I honestly feel for us to get the most out of life, we must learn to step out of our comfort zone and take some risk. I am not talking about life threatening risk either; the kind of risk that I am talking about is we must strike while the iron is hot metaphorically speaking of course. When you start to second guess yourself instead of going with your gut feeling, then you will be stuck in the same rut and start to feel like there is no way out. Some people at their jobs feel like there are no other opportunities awaiting them because they are either overthinking about jumping ship or start to second guess themselves when it has to do with their own abilities. I really feel that we must learn to take that necessary risk to make that change to our life for the better. It is just like a person becoming a Christian for the first time; that means that you have made the decision to follow God and do his will; that is a big commitment, but at the same time you are worried about what your friends will think. When I became a Christian in the year 2004, I knew that I had to make some changes to my life, and with me just being 15 years old that became apparent. Don't get me wrong I am not perfect by any means, but I do try to treat people right and follow God the best way I can. I done backslid a little bit, but like I said before I am not perfect, but God knows my heart. I had second thoughts about becoming a Christian at the age of 15, but I didn't let my overthinking become a deterrent.

We must also learn that we will be tested when making them positive changes to our life. Stressing over things that we do not have any control over is unhealthy physically as well as mentally. It gets tiring when it comes to stressing of uncontrollable things in life; that is why we must turn to God in prayer. Before God bless you, he will put you to the test rather you trust him that he will help you in certain situations or not. Following God and doing his good will according to the bible is not easy all the time; there is temptation out there that can come in between us and the Lord rather it is either sex, drugs, or any other worldly things that causes us to sin. Praying in the morning time when we get up and start our day is one of the most important things to do especially when dealing with stress in our lives. Life is not a joke by any means, so stressing over things that we don't have any control over can be overwhelming at times. It is always best to have that positive mindset and start your day off with a smile on your face because Jesus loves you and knows all about your struggles.

Another thing that we can use to counteract the stress is to focus on what we can control. We can control quite a few things such as our life, the way we view it, and how we can change it in a positive way. I honestly feel that if we have a breath in our bodies and God wakes us up in the morning, we still got a chance to make a change. We must also learn to be more optimistic and not complain as much.

The last thing that I will be talking about in this chapter when it comes to counteracting stress is taking a break from certain things. I am not saying just quit your job just because you are tired or just too lazy to work either; what I am getting at is we all need some time to recharge our batteries so to speak. I understand that you may be overwhelmed when working a dead-end job when there is no change for you to move up to either make more money or just trying to use your strengths to the best of your ability especially when talking about factory jobs. Factory jobs can and will have you stressing, but it is up to you to make changes to either your mindset going into work or just trying your best to move up. We also need to do a self-evaluation on ourselves when the stress is at an all-time high. Stress can kill you if not careful. I believe that couples take them vacations just because they need to escape the outside world sometimes; trust me if money wasn't no object, then I would take me a getaway vacation every quarter. I also believe that some of the reasons why people like their solitude so much is because you can escape the world even if it is just for a few minutes. I know personally that when I felt overwhelmed as a child or teenager, that I would just be either in my room playing video games or just outside playing by myself and to be honest I think that was part of my personal sanctuary. Remember, it is alright to work overtime and make some extra money, but it doesn't mean a thing when you don't make the necessary time to enjoy life while doing all that working.

CHAPTER

20

INVESTING IN YOURSELF

Sometimes in life, we must learn how to treat ourselves good by investing in ourselves. Investing into someone or something doesn't necessarily have to do with money all the time; it can be time, effort or just loyalty just to name a few things. Life is too short to not think about ourselves from time to time. As a good person, you may have let yourself go so someone else could be happy when you have helped them, however, are some of them people that you may have helped in the past thinking about you; that is often a question that we may ask ourselves time and time again.

We must learn to have love for ourselves so we can have it for someone else. Sometimes, in life you must be a little selfish for to be a success. I am not saying don't help people when they are in need; what I am trying to say is take care of yourself first before helping someone else. Investing in yourself is an important thing to do when making them life changes. It may be hard for some people because they may have been helping people all their lives, but not either getting the same thing in return or simply not used to thinking about what they need for themselves. Helping people in their time of need while you need help yourself can be an overwhelming trait to deal with. Sometimes, we must use our brain a little more than our heart.

One way to start investing in yourself is to start keeping a journal. A journal sometimes can be one of the tools that we can use to get out what we want to say or do. I personally keep a journal by writing down certain events that happen during the day that were eventful. Keeping a journal can also be like divine intervention because when people don't want to listen to you when you are trying to make conversation with them, then you can write what you are currently feeling and what you want to do with your life. When writing in a journal, it helps you escape reality even for just a few minutes. That is why a am a firm believer that certain books that people write can be based off personal experiences. We all experience life in different ways. You can also find solace when writing in a journal because you are at peace, and it is just you and God.

Another way to invest in yourself is trying to break bad habits that may be hindering you from making them positive changes to your life. We all have flaws and bad habits that can be overcome. Your positive mindset can be a major asset when trying to overcome a certain habit that you cannot simply shake from your life. Hanging with the wrong crowd can be a bad habit, but it can be overcome in time when trying to wean yourself from trying to join in the bad activities that they may want to do that can derail you from making them certain life altering changes. I really believe that my mother was too protective of me when going out with certain people, and in the long run it paid off. I am not saying that parents should pick the people that their children can hang out with, but I am saying that giving good advice to your kids is not a bad idea because at the end of the day, your kids are still your kids no matter how old they are. I was blessed to have the mother and the father figures that came along in my life that taught me right from wrong even though I didn't want to hear what they were talking about, but as I have gotten older, I begin to understand the things they were saying to me.

In addition to investing in yourself, we must get organized. Organizing certain things will be a benefit to the changes in your life that that you are trying to make. Organizing can be from just rearranging things around the house to just your thoughts. Not being organized can lead to problems in the long run because it can cause chaos and trouble for us. We must have some type of direction in life to go forward into them changes. It is just like you may be in a store and everything is well organized, and things are right where they are supposed to be. I personally hate walking into a store where everything is out of order, and nothing is where it should be. Life is about being organized; it is just like that old saying the cleanliness is next to Godliness. Investing in yourself is also being able to prepare for what you prayed for. I feel that being prepared and organized is one of the major things that we need to do for us to make it in this world. Think wisely when trying to be organize in life.

Finally, the last thing that I am going to talk about as far as investing in your self is to make a budget on what you want to do and how you are going to do it. Managing money can be hard sometimes, but it must be done when trying to invest in yourself. You may want to go out to eat every weekend with your friends, however at the same time you are trying to save up for a car; this is where the word sacrifice comes into play. It is just like you may want a new video game, but you know that you must buy groceries for your house; you make the decision that the video game can wait and go ahead and get the groceries for the house. When I was in college, I had to make plenty of sacrifices when it came to money because I couldn't just blow all my money on certain things that I can live without. I learned that I could go without either a video game or just going out to the club because I knew that my mother could only afford to send me so much money, so I had to spend it wisely.

I personally do not mind missing out on temporary fun, because when it is all said and done your money is gone and you have nothing to show for besides just the memory of just having a good time for just a little while. When you are on a budget, you must look at the bigger picture make the sacrifices that are needed to make it where you want to be in life. I have seen my mother firsthand make sacrifices for her children for us to have a great life and be happy. Like I said before life is too short to not try your best to be happy each day of your life. It took me four years to save up and get myself a car, but I made the necessary sacrifices to make it a reality. Remember, investing in yourself when it comes to changes to your life for the best is important because persistence pays off in the long run.

CHAPTER
21

CARE LESS OF WHAT PEOPLE MAY THINK ABOUT YOU

You may have heard the statement perception is reality at least once in your lifetime, and there is a lot a truth to that statement; the reason why I say that is because in life some people care about what their peers think of them. I honestly do not care about what people may think of me because no matter what I do rather it is negative or positive, people are going to have their opinion of me regardless.

The main thing I will be talking about in this chapter is not let anyone discourage you into making your own adult decisions in your life. When it comes to making certain decisions in life, no one can make the choices for you. You will have some people that may get in their feelings about the decisions that you make in life, but at the end of the day it is your life, and you pick and choose how it is going to play out. The future is what you make of it. Sometimes when making choices in life it can be difficult rather it is cutting out certain habits we may have or just getting rid of the bad influences that can derail us from making that choice to better ourselves.

When you start to care less about what people may think of you one of the things that you must learn is to expect and accept that people will have their own opinions about you regardless of what you say or do. I remember a time when someone was so disrespectful to me that it causes me to get out of character and snap on them because I have had enough. The aftermath of the situation was that I was called crazy and the person with the disrespect tried to put the blame on me and not speak to me over some stuff that they have done to me. I was always brought up to treat people with decency and respect, however I was also told not to tolerate disrespect from anyone. Some people will go a long time without speaking to anyone about rectifying the situation when they are in the wrong because it is either their ego or pride that gets in the way.

Like I said before, I am not above giving a

person an apology if I have wronged them in any kind of way. There are some people that are around my age that still act like children when it comes to either taking responsibility for their actions or just admitting to their wrongdoing towards people for no reason at all. Them are the people that we should try to avoid because they can either hinder us from taking that next positive step that we need to get where we are going in life, or we will be on that same level as them.

Everyone is entitled to their own opinion. I respect a person that will tell me the truth about myself straight to my face instead of just sugar-coating it so to speak because it helps me learn to do better. You are not going to like people's opinion about what they may say about you all the time; I mean that is life you are going to disagree on certain issues.

It is also important to know that everyone makes mistakes in life. I mean you are going to get those bruises and scrapes along the way. Anything worth having in life doesn't come easy; that is why we need to encourage and help each other because we all stumble and fall short. Making mistakes is part of growing up, but when you learn from them you do better. Do not let anyone tell you different when it comes to making mistakes because at the end of the day, we are all human and God understands that.

When it comes to caring less about what people may think of you, remember to love yourself and have the confidence to achieve your goals when it comes to changing your life. It is also important to believe in yourself that you will get the challenges that life throws at you because when it comes to defying the odds, it doesn't matter what other people may think of you because they are not living your life. I know that everyone may have heard the saying that when you walked a mile in my shoes you can tell me something; there is more truth to that statement than meets the eye. I really do not get that certain people are so quick to pass judgement on others when they do not know either their situation or dilemma.

In addition to what I am going to talk about in this chapter is practicing self-love and acceptance. Self-love is an important quality to have about yourself because it gives you the confidence that you can do anything that you set your mind to. I would be lying if I said that I didn't get down on myself, however I remained steadfast and had to remind myself that I am ok just the way that God made me. Sometimes I would get discourage just over anything behind closed doors in the comfort of my home; I mean I would either just sit in my car for about 30 minutes with my mind racing about certain things that might not be going right in my life or just in my house staring at the wall and being like why me. Even rich people get down on themselves from time to time when things start to crash down so to speak. We must remind ourselves that self-love is important to have in life.

There may be times that we may think that we are failing in life because either people got into our ear and said negative things, or it is just an emotional breakdown that we have from time to time. I even had people that didn't care about what I was feeling if they had someone to talk to or just try to use. Once they feel like that, they cannot use you anymore, then they don't want anything to do with you. Narcissists often feel like that if they see you weak, then they can manipulate you. When people think so highly of themselves like they are never wrong about anything, that is when the word arrogant comes into play. That is why it is important to stay away from people that play the victim all the time when they know that they are in the wrong because they are doing nothing more than being narcissistic.

The final thing that I will be talking about is not letting other people tell you what you can do that is positive in your life. Life is too short to let people undermine and discourage you from doing something positive. Certain people will discourage you for many reasons and the main one is that they do not want to see you doing better than them in life. Being envy of someone can be an ugly trait to have in your heart. I will be one of the first ones to admit that I have become jealous of things that either what some of the people I know had or just their life in general; then I realize that it was their season to have the things that they have or the life they are living, and in the back of my mind I knew that my time was coming because it says in the bible that there is a time for everything that is under the sun.

We must have a strong mindset when it comes to people that may be trying to either discourage or deter us from making them positive life changes. A strong mindset is one of the best assets to have when it comes to dealing with certain people that are trying to doubt your abilities. Adversity is a part of life that we must overcome to reach our goals. Remember, if we are persistent and have our faith that God will get the job done all of the hard work that we put into changing our life for the better will soon pay off and God will reward us abundantly.

CHAPTER

22

FINAL THOUGHTS ON EVERYTHING

Well, whoever is reading this book I hope your life is full of blessings and positive changes. For us to grasp on the word change, we must know what it means. I said before that I had a hard time dealing with changes rather it was when people switch up on me or just life in general; I learned at a young age that people will switch up on you and do not need a reason for it, so that may be the explanation for my trust issues but learning to be optimistic about certain things can help you become a better person.

You don't want to be a person that always have doubt in your mind because it will not propel you to success in life. Even though I am not fond of my current factory job, I try to make the best of it every day because any job is better than no job. I am just grateful for the people that are currently in my life in spite of what I have been through with some of them. I also had to learn at a young age that people are going to be people.

Like I said before, life is too short to care about a person's opinion about you because if I were to just sit down and worry about what people are saying and thinking about me, I would go insane. Always maintain your sanity even if it causes friction with your peers; at the end of the day, we are responsible for ourselves and our own actions, and with anything or anyone that is making you unhappy and creating nothing but chaos in your life, let it go.

Again, when you have been doing the same thing for so long, change can be a complex thing to go through. Change is not easy for everyone; it is something that we work at and adapt to every day of our lives. Every time when God lets you wake up in the morning, you have a chance to be better than you were yesterday because we can't get that day back. Never take anything for granted and make the most of every day. It is also important for us to try our best to live each day happy; never go to bed mad because life is like a vapor which mean we are here for a short period of time.

People interpret life in many ways; some people want to better understand it by either getting ahead or trying to better themselves. You also have the people that will put the blame on others because their life is all messed up. Like I said before, it is up to you to change your current lifestyle for you to be happy.

A lot of people play the blame game. The people that still play the blame game and not doing anything about the current situation that they may be in will not get anywhere in life because of their negative mindset. Certain people that were bad influences in my life I knew it became apparent that I had to isolate myself from them.

For the people that betrayed me, it made me

a better and stronger person because it made me more aware that anybody can turn on you. Don't sabotage your own happiness by trying to protect someone else's…. you'll lose every single time. Never let anyone or anything come between you and your happiness. Happiness is what most people want out of life and having that positive mindset can make it happen.

One of the most painful things that I had to go through when I was in elementary school was to watch all the other kids enjoy their grandparents-on-grandparents day because I felt out of place and dread that day so much. I think that personal experience that I encountered helped me become a stronger person because it did have a profound effect on my life because only my grandfather was still living at the time, and he lived all the way in Michigan. I am just glad I had a chance to meet him before he passed away. Albert Schweitzer once said, *"The true measure of a man is not to be found in man himself, but in the colors and textures that come alive in others."* This quote has a lot of truth to it because it is all about how we are supposed to treat people. That was the thing about my mother, she knew how to treat people right and I do my best the follow in her footsteps each day of my life.

In conclusion change comes from within; when it gets so that you are just tired of living in the same rut and having that negative mindset, you know it is time for a change. Change does not happen overnight; just got to believe in yourself and your craft. There is always a way out when you put God first and believe in him. There are times when our faith will get tested, and that is why it is important to remain steadfast. Some people thrive on adversity because it makes them stronger versus the people that will fold under the pressure.

In closing, I really hope that the people that are reading this book enjoy it; I am not and expert on certain topics like this one because I just go off or my personal experiences that I had in life.

There are a lot of positive things and advice to take from this book. My intentions are not to hurt people's feelings by any means by telling the truth and keeping it real.

Finally, stay true to yourself, believe, and be

persistent about the positive changes that you may

be trying to make in your life. May God bless you all

with a long and happy life full of blessings and

peace.

GOD IS GOOD.

TAKE CARE

About the author

I am just a guy from a small town in the state of Missouri that likes to write and chill with friends in my spare time life is too short to not be happy. I also like to play pick-up basketball games and just work on putting things together. I also have an associates degree in business administration. I do not claim to know everything, however the people that know me personally knows that I give the best advice that I can when it comes to treating people right.

Jerrell A. Gooden